FASHION LEGENDS ALPHABET

Words by Robin Feiner

Aa

A is for Anna Wintour. As Vogue's editor-in-chief, she's become one of the most forceful and influential people in fashion. No one dares cross 'Nuclear Wintour.'

B is for Manolo **B**lahnik. This superstar's gorgeous, elegant stilettos have strutted their way into fashionistas' hearts, making them true classics.

**C is for Christian Dior.
His curvaceous, 'New Look'
designs put Paris back at
the center of the fashion
world. Ooh la la.**

D is for **D**onatella Versace. Turning the family's business into an Italian fashion empire, it's impossible not to fall in love with her audacious designs and Medusa emblem.

E is for **E**lsa Schiaparelli. With creations like the Bowknot Sweater and the Shoe Hat, this visionary was a surrealist fashion rebel.

F is for Diane von **Fürstenberg.** This inspirational woman and legendary leader in the world of fashion, has her legacy all 'wrapped' up.

G is for **G**iorgio Armani.
As the inventor of tailored
red-carpet fashion, this
maestro has been crowned
Italy's most successful
fashion designer.

H is for Hubert de Givenchy. It is impossible to think of Givenchy without imagining the legendary black dress that Audrey Hepburn wore in Breakfast at Tiffany's.

I is for **I**ris Apfel.
This celebrated fashion icon hasn't let old age stand in her way, becoming more zany, flamboyant and famous with each year.

Jj

J is for Marc Jacobs. His style is a fresh mash-up of prep, grunge and couture. Some just call his look 'streetwise.'

K is for **K**ate Spade. Becoming a hit in the 90s, her sophisticated, stylish, and affordable handbags were so New York, darling.

L is for Karl Lagerfeld. Known for his distinctive white hair and starched collars, he is one of the most revered creative directors in fashion.

M is for Alexander **M**cQueen. With a flair for the dramatic, this British 'enfant terrible' gave us the 'bumster' jeans trend, and skulls ... lots of skulls.

Nn

N is for Helmut **N**ewton. This German-Australian photographer's bold black and whites, have made for some of the most dramatic Vogue covers, ever.

Oo

O is for Olivier Rousteing. At the age of only 25, this unknown designer took the reins of prestigious French house, Balmain. Sacré bleu!

P is for Miuccia **P**rada.
For this designer, business
woman and feminist,
success and iconic status
was 'in the bag.'

Qq

Q is for Mary **Q**uant. She popularized the miniskirt, hot pants and other controversial designs, making fashion fun for the young.

R is for **R**ei Kawakubo. As founder of Comme des Garçons, she believes in designing with the heart and constantly challenging herself to push fashion forward.

S is for **S**tella **McC**artney. Like her legendary parents, McCartney is a lover of animals, refusing to use them in the production of her clothes and accessories. Good mooooove.

**T is for Tom Ford.
A true creative force
responsible for reinvigorating
Gucci, building his own
label and even directing
amazing films.**

U is for King of **U**nderwear. Calvin Klein is the creator of so much greatness, but he will forever be remembered for his legendary, branded, white underwear.

V is for **V**alentino Garavani. Famous for his stunning dresses in "Valentino red," layers of white pleats and for even making leopard print cool.

Ww

W is for Vivienne Westwood. As a legendary 'punk' designer, she uses her influence to campaign for human rights and the environment.

X is for Alexander Wang. After only two years at fashion school, this Chinese-American designer launched his own iconic label. Take that.

Y is for **Y**ves Saint Laurent. This trailblazer gave us the women's tuxedo suit, popularized the beatnik look, and he was the first designer to use ethnic models. Props.

Z is for **Z**uhair Murad. This young, Lebanese designer has beauty and glamour all sewn up. Celebrities and their red carpets can't get enough of Zuhair.

FASHION LEGENDS ALPHABET
www.alphabetlegends.com

Published by Alphabet Legends Pty Ltd in 2018
Created by Beck Feiner
Copyright © Alphabet Legends Pty Ltd 2018

**EXPLORE THESE LEGENDARY ALPHABETS
& MORE AT WWW.ALPHABETLEGENDS.COM**